forage

forage

rita wong

Nightwood Editions
Gibsons Landing, BC

Published by Nightwood Editions
773 Cascade Crescent
Gibsons, BC, Canada V0N 1V9
www.nightwoodeditions.com

Cover design by Carleton Wilson
Cover photo ©LaiYun/Greenpeace
Author photo by Sita Kumar
Printed and bound in Canada

Nightwood Editions acknowledges financial support from the Government of Canada through the Canada Council for the Arts and the Book Publishing Industry Development Program (BPIDP), and from the Province of British Columbia through the British Columbia Arts Council, for its publishing activities.

This book has been produced on 100% post-consumer recycled paper, processed chlorine-free and printed with vegetable-based dyes.

Library and Archives Canada Cataloguing in Publication

Wong, Rita
        Forage / Rita Wong.

Poems.
ISBN 978-0-88971-213-3

        I. Title.
PS8595.O5975F67 2007   C811'.54   C2007-903871-9

in memory of 陳麥麗卿 女士

dedicated to her wisdom, courage & compassion,

& yours, interbeing

Table of Contents

lore/loose/lode

r

rr

rrr

rise

riven

rice

rrr

rr

r

value chain

how to turn english from a low-context language into a high-
     context language?

tomorrow and tomorrow and tomorrow takes me back hundreds
     of years

the internal frontier: my consumer patterns

what is the context for "you people are hard workers"?

electromagnetic fields of refrigerator, phone & computer hum
     bewildered static

cartons of cigarettes wait for lungs to reside in

heaps of dolls burn for the sins of their owners

sometimes i open my mouth and my mother's silences come
     tumbling out of me

"they take your culture away from you: you cannot sing your own
     songs anymore"

utter english, the terrain has altered & tong wa won't "fit" into the
     compartment allotted for it

so much depends on a thin iron wok

hello silent spring.

military industrial complex embedded in my imported electronics

offering

芝麻糊

faith hides in little pockets like the heart
& the throat. born with a serious streak
the width of an altar, i climb the stairs in
that first home, the zhi ma wu, black
sesame childhood sweet, squeeze soya
beans in a rough white cotton bag, hold
my mother's workworn hands. what do
any of these small gestures mean
except that they have carried me
into now? shadows in the corner.
dust on the shelves & in the blood. an
archival endeavour, let the fragments
stand together, make us larger than the
sum of the individuals. float from
quote to quote, to shore the body of
a man with hairy legs, a mi'kmaq
woman with dark hair who curls into
the sheets like a child, a gay boy who
made the best damn bannock i've ever
tasted. there's no justice for him to die.
ground to push against: red earth,
bloody earth, stolen earth. what the pen
takes, the throat can return.

catapult soil desert thrush grasses navigate skim the body's

planes. vessels throb on the stretch of skin transverse

trickle down: who wants sludge from the wealthy? tumbleweed western tumbledrawn

opium

chemical history narcopolemics
attempted genocide call it crack war
alcohol white powder suffocates
shades of deep brown earth red desert
yellow skin dependency myths who
needs the high of trying to kill the other?
racist gaze tingles on my skin induced
economic muscle flexes to displace
millions rifles fire behind the dollar
signs & still the underground pulses
suffering blue veins seek the
transformative heart as ordnance drops
on embassies & arteries cry for kin

"Queen Victoria waged war twice... in order to ensure the free commerce of opium."
— Avital Ronell

fluorine

arsenic in calculators, mercury in felt
hats, mad as a poisoned hatter
pyrophoric undercurrent in mundane
acts assume poison unless otherwise
informed crowded alloys detect no
health damage until generations later i
brush my teeth with nuclear intensity
the cavities i avoid destined for others
fall into hazardous-waste piles up as
i sleep smells though i don't see it
transported across oceans & into sad
rural neglect how shiny my teeth are
this cold crisp morning

"The vast majority of fluorine produced today is used in the nuclear industry." ($4F_6$)
—David Newton

trip

red bean black sesame soup baby
comes howling into this world
learns to eat every grain of rice
her first english word is no. NO. she
tumults through school years chases
dandelion whispers sharpens her
memory just for the ache of it. runs the
cash register with quiet aplomb. the leap
of faith into english an ocean in which
many have drowned. pacific immersion
eases the tone hungry heart momentarily,
but north by north undercurrent
language bobs within her, whetting her
dreams & lips, words come tumbling out
of her body, gather gravity's momentum
as she dreams children into exuberance,
villages into wakening, marks months by
dinners cooked & books read her internal
spark flourishes at the risk of external
combustion, always keep one eye to the
outer world, the way one fears & respects
a hungry tiger, the way dancer & dance
live in our rapidly thrilling throats, fill
each movement till the linger slips

the girl who ate rice almost every day

riceworld was sold out of brown rice so she went to the sundown mall on the street of no return. strolled past low maintenance, high risk properties in search of plump grains. distracted by gloss and air-conditioned spectacle, she said to the manager in the supermarket, what big beets you have.

all the better to tempt you with my dear, he replied. that most ungenerous of storekeepers frowned, for she had fingered his goods without purchasing them. try one, he urged, it's a free sample. the red sliver stained her lips, a cosmetic wound.

slow, for that was the girl's name, paused as she was wont to do. had these beets been crossed with cabbages to make them so huge? not cabbages but cows, replied the manager, with a drosophilic glint in his melanophore eyes.

oryza sativa inter alia

go to the US patent database, http://www.uspto.gov/patft and do the following search: search term: monsanto search field: assignee name a search of records from 1976 to january 2007 yields 3,894 records. if you add a second term, soybean, in the search field, title, you will find 210 patents.

if you change the second search term to rice, in the search field, title, and keep monsanto in the assignee name field, you will find 4 patents. corn yields 21 patents. tomato yields 2 patents. potato yields 2 patents. wheat yields 5 patents. cauliflower yields 1 patent.

dear reader, please note that these numbers are current as of January 2007; there is a high probability that the numbers will be greater by the time you access the database yourself.

the land of extinct animals was expanding exponentially, and she would be added to it too if she ate those beets, she realized too late. dangerous allergies and surprising properties made each object that crossed her lips an epiphany.

why, just yesterday, the oysters in the chiu chow congee yielded a small, imperfect pearl on her tongue. magic was all around her, had she the eyes to see it. corporate magic, crossing goats and spiders who had no desire to become one creature, pigs crossed with people until they collapsed under their own immense weight.

elm and larch trees offered her some comfort. their roots and the roots of their bach-flower sisters reached deep into the earth that would outlast her.

ah, but this was a story about rice. fluffy rice, hard, undercooked rice, white rice full of glucose waiting to enter the bloodstream, wild rice that turned the water purple with

US Patent 6,153,812: Rapid and efficient regeneration of transgenic wheat plants. Nov. 28, 2000. Inventors: Fry; Joyce Ellen (St. Louis, MO); Zhou; Hua-ping (Ballwin, MO). Assignee: Monsanto Company (St. Louis, MO).
"A rapid transformation regeneration system is disclosed. This system takes two–three months to obtain transgenic plants. Transformation efficiencies are very high. This system also has been demonstrated with several different selecting systems and is particularly useful for transforming wheat."

US Patent 5,663,484: Basmati rice lines and grains. Sept. 2, 1997. Assignee: RiceTec, Inc.
"The invention relates to novel rice lines and to plants and grains of these lines and to a method for breeding these lines. ... Specifically, one aspect of the invention relates to novel rice lines whose plants are semi-dwarf in stature, substantially photoperiod insensitive and high yielding, and produce rice grains

resistance, the rice that could be harvested three times a year in some parts of the world, and the brown rice that was her daily staple.

slow realized that she had been eating imported rice from china (white) and the united states of amnesia (brown) for most of her life. now that she had eaten the beets of no return, and did not have long to live on this earth, she wanted to know what a grain of rice grown on the land where she lived, the land of salish, musqueam, halkomelem speakers, would taste like? how could it grow? she determined to try to grow a small crop hydroponically.

she turned onto the avenue of final warnings and noticed a manhole cover that was ajar. peeking beneath, she saw a steel ladder that would provide entry into the sewers of her city. wet and warm, with occasional spots of light provided through the stained-glass sidewalks, the sewer had promise as a potential bed for her rice. she

having characteristics similar or superior to those of good-quality basmati rice.
Another aspect of the invention relates to novel rice grains produced from novel rice lines. The invention provides a method for breeding these novel lines. A third aspect of the invention relates to the finding that the "starch index" (SI) of a rice grain can predict the grain's cooking and starch properties, to a method based thereon for identifying grains that can be cooked to the firmness of traditional basmati rice preparations, and to the use of this method in selecting desirable segregants in rice breeding programs."

US Patent 6,229,072:
Cytoplasmic male sterility system production canola hybrids.
May 8, 2001. Assignee: Adventa Technology Ltd. (Sleaford, GB). "Our invention comprises a gene restorer line of Brassica napus which contains a Raphanus sativus restorer gene but is essentially free of Raphanus sativus genes which produce high glucosinolate.

enlisted the sewer rats to help her guard and cultivate this crop, by promising them half the yield, if it grew. her time was short, so she quickly tracked down some organic brown rice through ebay, which she used to seed the bed.

the beets had infused her excrement with a permanent red glow, but she still used it as fertilizer. the rice that grew from this experiment was rouged by the fertilizer, and became a sweet, rosy coloured grain that spread like a weed through the urban catacombs.

long after the last beet eaters disappeared from this spinning planet, the slow-cooking rice continued to make its way through the sewers and alleys of many a struggling city.

In particular, we provide a gene restorer line, and progeny derived therefrom, seed of which is low in glucosinolates...."

US Patent 6,498,285: Methods for producing transgenic pigs by microinjecting a blastomere. Dec. 24, 2002. Inventors: Ebert; Karl M. (Millbury, MA.
Assignee: Alexion Pharmaceuticals, Inc. (Cheshire, CT).
"*A transgenic large mammal is produced by a method including the steps of obtaining one or more early embryos, selectively preparing an embryo having at least three cells, and preferably at a stage in development corresponding in time to the onset of transcription of the embryo's paternal genome, and introducing isolated nucleic acid molecules into a blastomere of the selected embryo. The introduction of isolated nucleic acid molecules into such embryos results in the generation of transgenic large mammals at a significantly increased frequency...*"

nervous organism

jellyfish potato/ jellypo fishtato/ glow in the pork toys/
nab your crisco while it's genetically cloudy boys/
science lab in my esophagus/ what big beakers you have
sir/ all the better to mutate you with my po monster/
po little jelly-kneed demonstrator/ throws flounder-
crossed tomatoes / hafta nasty nafta through mexico,
california, oregon, washington, canada/ hothoused
experiment nestled beside basketballs of lettuce,
avocado bullets/ industrial food defeats nutrition/
immune systems attrition/ soil vampires call/ shiny
aisles all touch and no contact/ jellypish for tato smack/
your science experiment snack yields slugfish arteries
brain murmurs tumour precipitation whack

perverse subsidies

will pay for you to take my garbage away so i never have
to look at it, never have to imagine the roaches & rats
crawling through cucumber rinds, ragged underwear,
clumps of hair & crumbled up toilet paper. seagulls &
crows will feed on rotting leftovers, carrion will reek of
fetid life, full, wasteful, extravagant to extinction. fill my
car, our streets, with the corpses of iraqi civilians, the
ghost of ken saro-wiwa, the bones of displaced caribou.
it will clatter down the graveyard that masquerades as
a highway, emitting malaise to the tunes of eminem.
disaffect, reinfect me.

> *somewhere the small green*
> *weeds hover in the cement cracks, waiting to return earth*
> *to her rightful promise. somehow i will begin walking &*
> *bicycling for my life, for our lives, for the furry bats that*
> *await night's return, spring's diminishing secretions to*
> *revive & spill forth.*

cars, our computers, our Christmas tree lights all feed on photosynthesis as well, because the fossil

plants and animals that grew their bodies with sunlight." – Janine Benyus

fuels they use are merely the compressed remains of 600 million years' worth of

after "Laundry Song" by Wen I'to
Wash them (for the Americans), wash them!

from soapworn hands to toxic coughs
sputters patience rubbed too thin
the season of grease never ends but squeals
into perchloroethylene lesions
kidneys and livers mumble
to the brass of cash registers
ching chong rings
the water turned profit margin
laundered in endocrine disrupters
the sudsy chemicals gurgle fumes
sulk in your blood for a decade

you might carpenter a tree-house escape
but the assiduous rain will find your pores
one big inhale, washing washing
thyroid, chrysanthemums, duck eggs all together
from contaminated basin
onto tampered scale
for the checkout:
bark odes or bark owed
how to recompose clean lines
in body burden times?

聞
一
多

transcrypt

all the unspoken whys mountain and loom over us, all manner
of anger, all hurt & no heal, can't breathe fast enough to air such
creeping wounds, one blast, another sting, & so our predecessors'
flaws own us tirelessly, irefully, pulling us to our patient graves,
one fight after another, till it's over or we've passed this arsenal to
children to fire in the streets. *this is not the gift i want to be known
for. this is not the best gift i have to offer.* each moment, imperfect
yes, has a promise we more often break than not, yet stranger than
blood, most early in the morning, we taste star raw & ocean rise.
even as mercury accumulates, the tides replenish & revise our
policed shores.

the dance of the dutiful daughter

fracture capital

capture fractals

fractious carnival

curvaceous fraternal

fictitious carnivore

menstrual festival

favourite monsters

musclebound fencesitters

effeminate ministers

miniature effigies

efficient masturbation

monogamous ecstasies

equivocal mischief

ricochet

when the ship leaves the harbour, she hears the vomiting below. circling the ship, huge lanterns hanging from choppers. the ocean is angry. no, she is angry & blames the ocean. i can't bear the weight of history & i can't not bear it. when her clothes are burned, the stench sounds like canaries trapped in her throat. she knows she must make home up, tallying words & numbers into skeletons off which to hang her coat. the ship has left the harbour. it's not coming back. if i never see another ship again, it'll be too soon. when she yawns, the canaries flutter their smallest feathers. her breath smells of worms. until the melancholy becomes cholera, i do not know the name of this language. the shadow in the periphery would like to enter this room. why turn away? she only wants to rub her face against your faithless arm. tremble. ache. her name is slow. you have waited for her for a long time. why don't you look at her face? her gentle grimace. an anchor cold inside your belly. you don't know what she calls for because your ears are plugged against uterine howls of pain. when the dried clams became bloody soup, i smelled the harbour.

in for a penny, pound of flesh. crush the ginger. palm against the knife. smash the root wide open. her nostrils accept ginger. the air is in the kitchen. always carry a backup plan. garlic. flashlights. codes in case the cops are invading your privacy. until the root was smashed, i didn't know the sound of breakage. broken further than you knew you could. then break it again. the language that turns your verbs into nouns. messy accidents. argue incessantly if you have nothing better to do. noise levels are rising. be still my scared heart.

when the door opened, it was round. a moon. a woman in a moon. her gates wide open. just like that. the thresholds more vomiting the smells she refuses to name as if forgetting were its own solution. not a door today but a window. what are you saving the door for? don't you know that intruders are welcome? until the handcuffs appeared, she thought this place was benign if deluded. when the ship left the harbour something inside broke. there is no fixing this. the oceans will swell with prayers, flotsam landing in places you'll never see. you have more trust than you know what to do with. blessings & curses are cousins. her palm wide open. knife reverberates, tremor of her adamant tendons. when she looked up, the canaries had fluttered off to other homes. she was still piling up words like they were cages she could turn into nests. couldn't she learn from the birds? fractured like your entry into the language. why don't you pull the weeds out of your garden for the slugs to feed on? why does your grandmother keep sticking her hands in the crumbling earth? wary of her bony frame. sometimes you have to be approximate before you go precise. all intentions are dangerous. you know yet you still proceed. sharp objects cause bleeding. until i ate the sharp object, i didn't know it would slice the inside like so many question marks. hooks into syntax force of abortion. mammoth prints in the rumbling earth.

after "I Sing of Lienta" by Chẹng Min

nine seeds nursed in the midst of war
sprout a way of life
older than me, older than tv
small green cheers, bites of sunlight,
windsalt, rainsweep, lakewise, leafcries
what the tongue & jaws know:
some minerals can't be bought or pilled
reminders of hidden hunger
what nitrogen can't fix

mess is lore

the four-chambered heart braces itself

that onerous and onanistic organ pulsates

masticate and medicate through the machine's routine that
    weakens your spleen

tiny tributary from this human mulch

hurry makes you shallow (osho)

lucid or ludic at four in the morning, you are the descendant of
    soldiers, peasants and ginseng traders

let ego be unfolded like a pair of flannel pajamas

put your finger in my contrary

internal teratology, milk of origins

up the elevator, down the byzantine

awash in coping mechanisms and moping chemicals

ruminant and luminous

forage, fumage

from the georgia strait to the florida strait, it sounds so americanned

from the whulge to osceola, kissimmee, caloosahatchee, my tongue hovers over salishan, seminole words, hesitant & penitent

listen harder for a tone, a trace, trail

the tongue curls, words maimed fresh

excavate miami to find sweet water, that translation falters, begin again, from indians & cowboys to cocaine cowboys, the indians still here. the indians are still here.

in the united stakes of amnesia,* i enter a classroom: two-legged creatures from bangladesh, holland, jamaica, cuba, china, england, trinidad, colombia, peru sit together in a circle, carrying personal hells & rebel yells

how does one say *give back* in seminole? in salishan? route through the land's indigenous languages, bend inglish towards their spirits

verb the kanata, verb the ottawa, verb the saskatchewan, the manitoba, quebec, start in the middle of rupert's lament and work out, start from the coasts and work in, start

lament kneels, redress roams, navigate through hairshirts, armor, corporate crime, factory farms, invoke camaraderie's rough surfaces

lament, foment, reinvent

You're walking. And you don't always realize it, but you're always falling. With each step you fall forward slightly. And then catch yourself from falling. Over and over, you're falling. And then catching yourself from falling. And this is how you can be walking and falling at the same time.**

through the noise towards rhythm, contrapuntal village, not yet

the bridge was broken, so i fell into the swift flowing river

the undertow brought me to the strait of the spirit

where the river narrows

trickles, fills into the burial pit, cavernous continent

---

*Krisantha Sri Bhaggiyadatta
**Laurie Anderson
"It is not mere chance that the more inland provinces such as Quebec, Manitoba, Ontario, and Saskatchewan bear Indian names while the maritime provinces or external coastal zones such as Newfoundland, Prince Edward Island, Nova Scotia, New Brunswick, British Columbia and Northwest Territories carry names with European origins. The political economy of conquest and trade can give more detailed answers than philology" (Marwan Hassan Velocities of Zero 107).

Kebec : Algonquin for where the river narrows

Manitoba : Cree for strait of the spirit

recognition/identification test:

crocus

holly

bamboo

magnolia

rhododendron

azalea

cedar

willow

eucalyptus

foxglove

pine

lavender

pansy

hemlock

dill

sage

arbutus

dogwood

blackberry

nike

pepsi

BMW

macdonald's

benetton

safeway

sony

chevron

KFC

pfizer

ipod

lipton

nestle

walmart

shell

esso

adidas

disney

blackberry

one remedy from a long series of remedies

(diagnosed by Jenny Ma)

白术　　　bai zhu   *rhizoma atractylodis macrocephalae*

茯苓　　　fu ling   *poria*

鸡血藤　　ji xue teng   *caulis spatholobi*

山药　　　shan yao   *rhizoma dioscoreae*

甘草　　　gan cao   *radix glycyrrhizae*

桑寄生　　sang ji sheng   *herba taxilli*

制何首乌　zhi he shou wu   *radix polygoni multiflori preparata*

麸炒枳壳　fu chao zhi qiao   *fructus aurantii preparatum*

党参　　　dang shen   *radix codonopsis*

language (in)habits
from and for UH

the gap between the crying line & electric speech
is the urbanization of the mouth
round peasant dialect vowels relocate
off the fields into city streets
where sound gets clipped
like our ability to smell the wet earth
sound becomes wound
we look away from toisan ache
ears fill with transience
ears like automatic cars blasting cantopop
forget the surprise of lungs & tears
wails, lunges, and the nightly irrelevance of traffic lights
bodies slowing & speeding up regardless
of what the signal tells us

電話

up on the language habits of the group." – Edward Sapir

open the brutal

                                 your coast in my
marine. my still eye in your hurried
claim. rupture abundance. loosen the
literal to littoral. slippage is better than
nothing, squirrel running across the
grass, a living question mark bounces
black & feisty before my eyes. Keep
moving like that squirrel, faster than the
guard dog chasing it. change the shape
of the slot slide it somewhere looser.
your teeth a serif that hooks my ear.
loose hair flutters debris in the night.
lyric is not rule but desire's lock.
signpost the revolution. your body's
alphabet encrypts the message. rising,
sigh the silent letter that alters the
sound around it. flesh holds fine blue
lines hiding just below skin, a small
wrinkle drafts years of battles &
bedrooms into its fold. drafts me
into your likely fire

canola queasy

vulture capital hovers over dinner tables, covers hospitals a
sorrowful shade of canola, what gradient decline in the stuck
market, what terminal severity in that twenty-year monopoly
culled the patent regime, its refrain of greed, false prophets
hawk oily platitudes in rapacity as they engineer despair in
those brilliant but foolish yellow genetically stacked prairie
crops. how to converse with the willfully profitable stuck in
their monetary monologue? head-on collisions create more
energy but who gets obliterated? despite misgivings i blurt,
don't shoot the messy angels with your cell-arranging blasts,
don't document their properties in order to pimp them.
the time for business-as-usual died with the first colonial
casualty. reclaim the long now. hey bloated monstrosity:
transcribe your ethics first or your protein mass shall turn
protean mess and be auctioned off in the stacked market and
so you can reap endless cussed stunts.

---

*Dedicated to Percy Schmeiser, the Saskatchewan farmer harassed
and sued by Monsanto because genetically engineered canola blew
into his fields.*

"In April 1997 Monsanto pulled two varieties of genetically engineered canola seeds from the Canadian market after testing

revealed that at least one of the patented herbicide-tolerant transgenic varieties

contained an 'unexpected' gene. This was after 60,000 bags of the seeds had already been sold throughout Western Canada." - Mae-Wan Ho

chaos feary

pyre in pirate bio in bile
mono in poly breeder in
womb pull of landrace allo
me poietic auto me diverse
trans over genic harassment
over seas genetic as pathetic
as engine of disease socio
me catastrophe political and
eugenic organ as an ism
general as the mono startle
of a soma ethic under
trodden patent as in lies
hubris as in corporate
coalition as in american
military as a choking tentacle
as pollution erodes these lines
no sense in food or rhyme
resistant as in herbicide or
people lost and found field a
factory dinner a roulette
conquest as in seeds hands as in fist

upon reading Biopiracy by Vandana Shiva

23 pairs of shoos
a response to Kathy High

the scientists are invested
& corporations even more so, directors of protein pipelines

we are closer to pigs and flies than we ever realized
bless their rapidly mutating souls

the convict may get his revenge
jernigan's thorax all over the internet while the housewife
                remains anonymous

faster, faster, faster
do it because you can

overdetermined and undermined
she nonetheless navigates with her ripped-up, ragged map

would you like a boy or a girl in your womb?
maybe spring for the hermaphrodite special

suppose steve kurtz tried to spread the wealth
the FBI is there to serve and protect the pipeline directors

child of ARPANET
resides on my fingertips

analyse the fingernails
to find out if she's queer

heel today, gall tomorrow
the empire's leprosy, gaia's rot

trading in futures
for winnowed pasts

how vigilant, how round
lysosomes confound

modify our birth certificates
to assert self-sovereignty over our genes

free trade or free will
can you tell the rhetorical difference?

she walked right past her offspring
without knowing

fly-by-night
fetuses, inc.

give it up
for adoption

the market is determined
by the demon hand, demand

the child
could refuse

how do we measure
emotional crops?

wombs
unite

the unconscious
rises in my throat

drag the child along
despite itself

snipstream

in the city of mass condo construction
social housing shortages continue

thrill seekers and pill eaters are hereby notified:
"Missing feedback is a common cause of system malfunction."*

the turn from canwest aspers towards lebanese bloggers
discloses the back door of gated communities: favelas

would she talk like this if she were born into reality tv shows?
the inner gambler suspects she would

the crowded body hosts a committee meeting:
inner chide, murderer, prostitute, witch, buddhist nun all
        convene

what we learn from a day at the races:
realign the racetrack in a marxian manoeuvre

"Adding or rerouting information can be a powerful intervention,
        usually easier and cheaper than rebuilding physical
        structure."*

credit or debit, they ask. the hidden three percent
accumulates with trust-use cards, awaits reattribution

Donella Meadows, "Places to Intervene in a System"

stance

scavenger, nomad, guerrilla-in-training, she surfaces against
the iron tide, wave's collapse against her cheek, undercurrent
tugging distress from its grainy shallows, sundering the view from
above, scatter cross-purposes, dishevel domination, destination
undecided. derivative forces intimidate but scatter continues,
anarchy fluctuates her muscle corpuscles circulate with skeptical
love in a body politic with revolt. provincial explosions, global
implosions, a stretched girdle, a timely meridian, an undone song.
she whistles the street's poverty to unpracticed ears, the corridors
of power noisy with mistakes, alleys pumping a moral exhaustion,
she resounds.

domestic operations

the home's plaintive cry
upon being invaded by CNN:

> *When the rich declare war, it is the poor who die.*

unable to bear the wart on error,
war-torn era, warped shorn blare on
living room as fractured as the globe
in the hands of the arms manufacturers
running the commercial breaks

      nuclear spectres

empty of hawks, doves, wrens, sparrows,
nests shaken by contrail, red, white & blown-apart
twigs scatter like bones across the unhomely ground

      a walled mind becomes a coffin

ears register the wails of orphans unbroadcast
the corpses 'democracy' won't see in that unblinking stare,
that glazed look called mass media

the screen, strident with what it excludes
from the televised parade of patriotism,
struck with military hypnosis,
disguises the very ground it violates,

      all our relations

For Carol Gilbert, Jackie Hudson, Ardeth Platte, three Dominican sisters who disarmed a missile silo in Colorado on Oct. 5, 2002, the anniversary of the US bombing of Afghanistan. Acting out Isaiah's prophecy "they shall beat their swords into ploughshares," the three nuns hammered

domestic operations 2.0

the eagle will plummet if one religious wing refuses to hear the other religious wing. intimidated by the testosterone in suits but refusing to back down. the state of the world precariously perched on some republican fingertip. middle finger. maybe a liturgical reminder. maybe humour. maybe denial. maybe a miracle cradled in skeletal hands. suddenly a bureau, tilted, falling, collapse. the furniture of our discontent. supplied a collective cave. the collapse of empires. when cottage industries return, what about the trees? will i speak the dialects of leaf, branch, wind? wet earth calls forth my maternal instincts. do the suits have maternal instincts? sure could use an estrogen bomb aimed at the pentagon right about now. a betty crocker takeover even. housewives of suburbia unite, you have nothing to lose except your lives if you wait any longer. an apron of discontent. a whole refrigerator full. replace the steroid-laden steaks with happy cows and more vegetables. replace cancer with sinewy health. why not. from apathy to anarchy in a few consonants. somehow witness does not equal resignation. locating hope in the unpredictable and the shared. assembling to conjure up a larger spectre than fear. larger than greed. larger than marx even. sudden bearded lady apparitions. missile apprehensions. monstrous attention scarlet alert weather and consumption patterns transform property into commons.

on the concrete silo lid, cut cables, spread their blood in the sign of the cross on the silo tracks and completed a liturgy before they were surrounded by armed military personnel. They were arrested and imprisoned in the Clear Creek County Jail in Georgetown, Colorado.

fester

fettered
       fetid
  fervid   trade
                              traitor
ferocious trade
       trap

      f u e l
                  fink trade
      f e u d
               f kt e

       gravytrainhasleftthestation

sweatshoparoundyourthroat

                      discounts your mother

supplant and command ordains the invisible hand

damage

people walk around in various states of damage. damaged goods. mismanaged funds. poverty rampage in corporate attire. let them eat mutual funds. the rate of interest is ejaculatory. eleven dribbles into two. murderous profit margins. mowing the law. moaning the lost. manning the last *financial post*. when did i become a commodity? a calamity? indemnity? the trend to credit facilitates fascism. ATM: automatically tracks movement, a totalitarian market, antagonize the machine & see what happens. waiting for goliath. the slingshot has become a teddybear catapult. slapsuits on everything from burgers to cartoon mice. the disney empire no laughing matter, laughing master. lasting mistakes. would kafka wear nikes? hand-me-down reeboks? a profound mistrust of fashion is healthy. your insecurities are showing. disco famulan gives me a headache. on a coca-cola campus, you learn crud. pepsi pisses me off. hasn't all that sugar caused enough damage already? walk around in sodapop stupor, consolidated carnage. a big burp would be a start. chapters chatters a tale of diminishing returns, nonchalant dirge for small presses. moaning the lost while the laughing master steals more. where's my slingshot?

Written post-FTAA protests in Quebec City, 2001.

sort by day, burn by night

circuit boards
                    most profitable & most dangerous
if you live in guiyu village,
one of the hundred thousand people who
                                "liberate recyclable metals"
                                        into canals & rivers,
                            turning them into acid sludge,
                                        swollen with lead,
                        barium leachate, mercury bromide.
            o keyboard irony: the shiny laptop
            a compilation of lead, aluminum, iron,
plastics, orchestrated mercury, arsenic, antinomy…
                            sing me the toxic ditty of silica:
        "Yet utter the word Democratic, the word En-masse."*

where do metals come from?
where do they return?
                    bony bodies inhale carcinogenic toner dust,
                            burn copper-laden wires,
                        peer at old cathay, cathode ray tubes.
            what if you don't live in guiyu village?

what if your pentium got dumped in guiyu village?
your garbage, someone else's cancer?

economy of scale
shrinks us all

global whether
here or there
collapses cancer
consumes en-masse

---

*Walt Whitman, "One's Self I Sing"
Upon watching the video Exporting Harm, http://www.ban.org/

trickledrown infect

intermittent insistence sinister complicity stillborn mister minister toxic tinctures stinking pistols stricken cysts or cynical sisters strychnine biscuits kiss or desist lore please pucker up and miss or responsible for which mess your dissatisfaction resists bores goriness consists of not cleaning up your mess for centuries nor paying your debts to those you've made poor with your thefts sir

spoken over so

poked on avowals imp hailed by syntax stick men
or skinny women struck by what big eyes you have or hand-ear
coordination provocation for the messes let them eat spam gum up
the incoming male with viagra offers or wired funds from nigeria
but they remake themselves with minutemen on steroids rifled or
stifled by earth's evacuation capitalist accommodation predation
predicament upturn or acid burn up st. louis misery turn tofu into
pharmachemical product DNA stranded this episode of the slit
episome is interminable welcome to evolutionary fumble as seed
sponsorship falters

chinese school dropout

scribble a tree
mouths piled up for height
announce a yellow belly
full of field

simplified characters
drift without context to anchor them
pearls washed upon deltas
clamhappy or oystershy, red tide?

cultivate nets
for scavenge repurposing
reinvent emperors & beggars
barefoot doctors, bartering mothers

water buffalo meander
chickens scramble dirt
banana trees shudder
guava release

boiled-water advisory
thermos dependency
sweat festival
cantonese cleanse

shoulder pole suspension
dumpling vendor
pancake roaster
taxi entrepreneur

noodle maker
rice boiler
frog catcher
dream crater

new puppet show
old opera story
costumed courage
pear gardens, peach thieves

shenzhen hallucinates
disposable factory girls
lucre impoverishes
stories go underground

green trust

frail leaves run tawny on the cement road robust insects fill the earth's crevices, deliver protein and crumbs to further staunch the already drying water table. aquifers decline and benzene creeps into the water supply. why learn the word benzene? so as to not choke on oil and gas, hoping for wind and wave and sun and tide to climb, remember moon's wax, crawl into tomorrow's basement with divination hunkering in the lumbar. sunken and pulled into irregular baskets, shaven and smoothed into bare warm skin, i looked under the table for childhood monsters and found an empty room, ladies in waiting and scholars long vacated, reconstruction moved to the cavernous library, each breath filling my nostrils with drunken nostalgia and sober, pale grapes. the crumbs piled up, large as stacks of unread newspapers. the electricity bill surged. hydro hailed us. wind witnessed our vespers. conditioned air merged with my neighbour's television and the unheard clock. in the hot stickiness i looked hard for my nutshell, cracked just enough to admit a stubborn moon. ants crept and crawled for mercy and sustenance. geckoes fed on the ants. i could not shut out traffic, noise would enter by any means possible and a light embrace might be more satisfying than turning the other sheaf or slapping dead the intruders. the dull whir of the bulldozer stopped for lunch. intermittent hammering chimed steady and industrious. the next shift may be the biggest one yet, the union of the living, from mosquito to manatee to mom.

"our past goes on living through us" –roy kiyooka

words pile up like rubble: liberate democracy freedom.
if oil in the pipelines would explode. what ignition turns
the sugar in the apple pie black? the quick burn of too
much patriotic carbon. dolorous banana republics. cavities
accumulate. newsprint wobbles, flag wavers in the distance.
turning pages rustle greased dereliction. financial traction,
troubled fictions. mouthing the wholesome script of the
war criminal. My lips blacken bitter with prime-time lies.
dominant is as dominant does. glucose glutton daddy, hedge
your money on a barter economy.

interchanges english/chinese,
handwritten margined notes
footnotes

"We are a people tending toward democracy at the level of hope; on another level, the economy of the nation, the empire of business within the republic, both include in their premise the concept of perpetual warfare." –Muriel Rukeyser

vessels

prison
health

subterranean creatures shudder in radioactive throes. my ears have filled with so much dust, my fat infused with flame retardants. scientists can't tell how the PBDEs entered me. bioaccumulative means you & me, baby. misery loves cacophony. the little crab might scuttle by, not a green rock to be found. i am bewildered by the organized violence of the prison, its sterile concrete and buzzing doors mock me. glass booths. blind gaze. the tepid dissection of the control room. bleached floors. impermeable surfaces. soulgrinding tedium. what books could hatch in that dull coffin? in its stingy confines, human appetite is surveilled—instant noodled—discarded. its life cycle has a crinkly plastic sound followed by a metallic titter. unbearable waste. no making without destruction. if debris could fly. with guardian disdain or guardian condescension, the locks are automatic. authoritarian paternalism begins & ends here. erroneous centres fall apart. suicides & segregation torture. the unit locked down. overdose & underwhelm. the body count automatic. the meds are administered on time every night. if reading can save even one life. one loose woman somewhere in the bowels of the obscene "correctional centre." who criminalized survival? the life you steal might be your own.

—ray kiyooka ... *passassod sip*

p a r e n t (h) e t (h) i c a l   b r e a t h
from & for RK

if these cells ever absorb the warmth of an Indian autumn:
perambulatory witness to neo-colonial streets in saltwater city,
Aboriginal Columbia, this year of increasing immune system
disintegration

a pulmonary commons called planet

a breath that met another in the commotion of nouns, gerunds,
subordinate clauses cluttering the historical air: *whoo-oosh!*
ping!

urban smog doesn't obscure empire smash, just clings to its
paraphernalia, obdurate rem(a)inder

dene becomes need if you throw off regulation, peregrinatory
realignments incant

holy need chirps on these wintry pages, migratory passages
looking to make "generosity of method" homing pigeons to
carry unrelenting songs

'all the peoples comprising the far-flung 'dene nations' keep having their entitlements shoved under the bureaucratic

red carpet... If History can be said to 'mean' anything for the likes-of-us, it must

surely mean that those who in everyway preceded us [...] have a claim upon those of us who were...So recently

55

on encountering trouble

"The black cottonwood is the third plant, after rice and a weed called *Arabidopsis thaliana*, to have its genome sequence published."
–*The Globe and Mail*, 14/09/06

stoke the ice tray's freezer burn; is this cause for confiscation? oryza rails, don't call DNA "junk" because you can't tell what it does. lignin declines to resist. ocean pout scheduled to enter your ice cream in 2008, unlabelled dietary supplement. mouse-ears shiver close to the contaminated ground. a ninefold wonder we haven't collapsed yet, towers of manufactured consent continue to broadcast blowhards, commercials plait themselves into our waking dreams, jingles, trigrams, stubborn surprises, swampy sedges, your best guesses cut through binary operations to sprout street cred, reconcile old enemies into symbiotic systems   troposphere's big belly hurricane hiccup down the beachfront lifts parrots out of conservatories, genetically engineered corn out of shipping containers, and fast food out of test tubes. when did short grains & long gains stop being seeds?

science vs traditionalism

Voices are likely to be activists + scientists poets theorists

after "The Stars" by Ping Hsin

adorn the railroad tracks
with fragile offerings:
incense, oranges, hemp hell money
fashion blades of grass into brooms
to sweep the ancestral hearth
fold apologies and rice paper prayers
into small organic boats
to send downstream
no more dioxins, no more
exponential mistakes
magnifying their way up the food chain
into my mother's thyroid
my neighbour's prostate
my cousins' immune systems
my aunties' breasts
my grandmother's cervix

冰
心

after fire carriages have ripped through
sweetgrass, sage, canyons, crags
wrecked indigenous homelands
tore coal out of mines
drained water from wells
sacrificed celestials every mile
more disfigurement than development
we summon precautionary principles
in agriculture, manufacture
voluntary simplicity
coyotes bare their sharp teeth
have the last howl

reconnaissance

habitual placement of the tongue changes the mouth.

when the tongue is still, are you quiet enough to hear the dead? quiet enough to hear the land stifled beneath massive concrete? quiet enough to hear the beautiful, poisoned ancestors surfacing from your diaphragm?

i don't want a lawn. i want a forest. the path to the treehouse is unpredictable. i couldn't stand the click of locks, the turn of keys that won't work. the promontory shivered, the peninsula reigned. the mountain was a turtle waiting for the sun to warm its back. the carp ate the crumbs of tourists with instinctive gulps. the water rippled until i could no longer see myself in the pond.

the tongue cooled with the breeze i blew against the hard palate. what languages do you arm yourself with?

verbs that occur in the present tense 80% of the time: bet, doubt, know, matter, mean, mind, reckon, suppose, think
verbs that occur in the past tense 80% of the time: exclaim, eye, glance, grin, nod, pause, remark, reply, shrug, sigh, smile, whisper
–*Longman Student Grammar of Spoken and Written English*

"it is not possible to add pesticides to water anywhere without threatening the purity of water everywhere. Seldom if ever does Nature operate in closed and separate compartments, and she has not done so in distributing the earth's water supply. Rain, falling on the land, settles down through pores and

豈有此理！ hei yow chi lay!

the turtle shrugged into its hard palate, an overlooked lesson on long term planning.

intent upon the elevator, she missed the roof. the best place for the tongue to rest.

"A new Chinese working class is struggling to be born at the moment when the language of class is curtailed and becomes inarticulate. The new working class is this spectral other, gazing at itself but expecting no one else to see it. An orphan's fate is its misery as well as its luck."
–Pun Ngai, *Made in China*

even orphans have ancestors. lungs become lunges when you make more space for their words.

the reigning voice resigns or resignifies

ipperwash, gustafsen lake, oka, burnt church, port radium, nitassinan, lubicon lands: returning to the scene of the crime, which you never left. *natives land*

cracks in soil and rock, penetrating deeper and deeper until eventually it reaches a zone where all the pores of the rock are filled with water, a dark, subsurface sea, rising under hills, sinking beneath valleys. This groundwater is always on the move, sometimes at a pace so slow it travels no more than 50 feet a year, sometimes rapidly.

hyper-capitalism is not just annoying but deadly

some dreams are trances

the american trance

annoyance is a warning signal

corporations eat the poor and spit out their bones

nisga'a land

the amount of weaponry correlates to the level of guilt

obscene wealth is not earned but stolen

i counted sweatshops in vancouver's eastside until i got dizzy and
fainted

assume spiritual plenitude – can you?

she stumbled through the mall in a consumerist trance
until she decided to slice up her credit card in time to the muzak

lubicon land

cree first nations

by comparison, so that it moves nearly a tenth of a mile in a day. But mostly it contributes to streams and so to rivers. Except for what enters streams directly as rain or surface runoff, all the running water of the earth's surface was at one time ground water.

irresponsible displacement of imperialist guilt causes massive
deaths
is psychobabble for: learn to share

fiscal this and fiscal that

hand over fist

market forces

the captains of industry don't feel guilty about wealth because
they share the guilt

uranium nightmares, cobalt collusion

rearrange molecules through thought not genetic engineering

coast salish land

prisons R not us

violent deportations from this state
announce imagi-nation's failure

a desert waiting for your wisdom

think potlatch

And so, in a very real and frightening sense, pollution of the groundwater is pollution of water everywhere." ~Rachel Carson

이 경 해

李 京 海

**for Lee Kyung Hae
Korean farmer
martyred in Cancun
(1947–2003)**

WTO
smashes rice farmers into
the enduring earth

but your sacrifice
invokes capitalism's fall
so earth resurges

gift economy
socialism's red fist unclench
open palm stories

*martyr to antiglobalization
movement.*

destructive effects of free trade

may you be graced by camaraderie with Navdanya, Wild Moon Rice, Hou T'u…

后土

resilience, impure, forms

the neighbourhood continues
on furniture and flutes, steam baskets and chinese tamales

vessels maintain & trim, all husk & hue, hollow & watertight
till a crack lets the light in everything

an anthem's shadow dispels the corporate spin
but the microchips still tie me in

"people become very similar in terms of their purchase
            decisions"*
where's a little privacy hedge in an electronic monoverse?

shiny gadgets and cookies notwithstanding
might i kneel in the nursery every day, touch earth,
or get swept & swooshed away in a virtual flood

haptic tactics counter video glare
wield torches, walking sticks & talking sticks

seek catamaran, trellis, suspension bridges, ropes, crutches
chew on sinew, tread gingerly on mycorrhizal mat

o sing of panda food and complex mats, teahouses and smooth
      handles
o sign of rainforests, lignification, silica, dense clusters

from electric shadows to forestly shade
pulp, flesh, bear witness to how breath seeks tree

may branches hold and restore marbled murrelets,** ducks, geese,
shelter ibises, grateful swallows, egrets, peace

---

*Kenichi Ohmae
**With gratitude to Uts'am and hope for the murrelets' survival.

after "Thinking of a Fair One" (si mei ren)*

little pilgrim culls friendship from the computer screen, plucks emails from electricity, botany's archaeology from search engines: dwarf figs, wild parsley, sweet orange blossom. cheeks suffused with virtual glow, she asks the march of letters for her silicon fortune. tap tap tap, draw yarrow sticks and preserved plums from the ming jar jpg. mouth opens, hands omen, see where they land. tap tap on laptops whose manufacture churned sludge into rivers and watersheds. return of the unrest: leap kung fu matrix morph orpheus into office cubicles, restore justice to the virtual workplace, seeds to the squirrels, bamboo leaves to clean water, free for all

Songs of the South: An Anthology of Ancient Chinese Poems by Qu Yuan and Other Poets

l

ll

lll

lore

loose

lode

lll

ll

l

easy peasy

a big bratwurst for my sister she likes them
meaty these days omnivorous sibling
spelunking and kneeling rapt and
unwrapped fried and untried nude and
disguised smooth and surprised
two eggs on the side an omelette
she cried more sauce for the ride
and hotter next time

susurrus

the days passed by in fear & uncertainty

the days passed by in caffeine & deadlines

the days passed by in crunchy textures

the days passed by in an irritable striving for carnal knowledge

the days passed by like sluggish cats

the days passed by like a mosquito whining for blood

the days passed by downloaded MP3 turned into a vlog

the days passed by in rice-cooker steam, diffusing a soft crust on
the wall

the days passed by like shadows in my closet, barely disturbed by
the rattle of hangers

the days passed by like constipation

the days passed by under the shingles of the communal house,
temporarily sheltered from UV rays but riddled by bird shit

the days passed in endless lists of tasks to do

the days passed by, all lassitude & turpitude, serpentine &
     labyrinthine

the days passed by in ritualistic meetings

the days passed by like a swig of beer ends up in the toilet

the days passed in the hum of electronic appliances punctuated
     by the sproing of the computer being turned on

the days passed by in email backlog

the days passed by like a repurposed stock market

the days

the days

the days

powell street

biking down the august streets of vancouver i find my pride at powell street. reverberating into the crowd as exuberant taiko. walk into a sea of issei, nisei, sansei pride, generations of pride playing in rock bands, doing park clean-up, serving corn on the cob, making videos, doing a post-atomic dance. loud, juicy watermelon smashed open pride. lazy summer sweet, sweaty orange pride that turns your quick stride into a languid prowl. an icy lemon kakikori pride, melting on my thirsty tongue. once found pride somewhere on the curve of her nape, on the pout of her lips, in the welcome between her thighs. now i rummage through the ashes looking for stubborn, black swishy strands of girl pride recently shaved off. a bare nun pride. a coldblue tightlip heartbruised pride that holds your shoulders rigid, your back sad. pride on salish land. kaslo, slocan, new denver, greenwood, black & white archived internment survival pride. ragged ass bi any means necessary random trigonometries of pride. oppenheimer park downtown eastside strung out on the street scowling pride. oxymoronic cop in a uniform pride. not just the usual suspects, the flashy buffed fag dancing on a float or glittery drag queen strutting pride but a burnaby correctional centre prisoner pride, a mom and dad marching in PFLAG pride, an every day in high school pride, elementary pride, endless legal battles to win pride, child-friendly pride, a jenny shimizu is everywhere hello kitty hello pussy pride. kiss me like you mean it pride. finally coming out to your momma pride that is actually relief. scavenging alleys for art materials pride. creating our own rituals because we need to pride. give me graffiti pride over the glossy commercial brand any day. a constantly inventing what we desire

---

With acknowledgements to Adrienne Rich whose words help close this piece.

acute

a fiery triangle needs big chunks of log, not small kindling to keep it steady through the night's chill. she learned the importance of proportion – big heat from big risk, a heart as large as a house warmed by risk. heat rises and it doesn't look back. in the cool aftermath the frogs gurgle a reminder of betrayed bodies. the triangle keeps burning. she sleeps on stiff cotton alone these nights. awakens to windows full of lake. listens for the sound of stone. hears trees creak a careful warning. such a difference a couple branches can make. tongs to stab the burning hearth.

elbow jab

dragracing from the foothills hospital to the earls on 16th intimate parking lot moments and crowchild trail automatic you held those virgin moments in your politicized heart after the rhetoric and principles had cleared you were a chinook hovering over nosehill park a shadow waiting for the lambda supermarket to be built detours to rooks to herland to take back the night your version of this city tiptoed on lubicon solidarity when the spirit sings skidded with tsuu tina siksika stoney histories that emerged like long anticipated rain from dry colonial oblivion you were a creature of extremes from drought to blizzard you were thirsty for spring what dandelions could bring when the third chinatown finally took root where the distance between the cultural centre and the native friendship centre could be measured in feet how many steps to cross the lioned bridge you could spit into the river you were so close you were in the back seat of that old station wagon looking out over the bend before the windows fogged over and the inner city libraries closed down the hospitals too before the liquor stores grew more numerous than schools you were sad for the city of your first wry love

precipice

dive thru oceans of sleep
                follow amber autumn, sing
                                the grip of sleeping tiger hills
feline earth in frozen pounce
                  when the rumble comes,
                                dive for cover!
adrenaline memory
                decolonizes cartilage
                              with queer precision
learn magpie vernacular
                chrysanthemum chronicles
                              robust rhizomes
make offerings
                appease the cranky grannies
                              with earth dumplings
curcuma ochre
                cedarwood incense
                              prairie sage
green rooftops
            community garden composts
                          pedal bicycles to save polar bears

aftermap

i don't follow & i don't lead. i was
never meant to dance in that strictly
defined way. body bobs upstarts its
own rhythms & upsets, small storms a
daily occurrence. yet somehow we
danced as though we could meet &
breathe the same air. your hand, my
back, like butter on bread, we were
morning familiar the moment we
met. click. in your presence i dance
on tabletops. click. can't follow you,
never could, you are like an
amputated arm, still feel your
presence long after your removal.
can't bandage this up. you instigate
the storms that move me along still.

resuscitate

could sleep for centuries until you break my skin, draw up my mutinous juices, could lie fallow and expectant, dormant through winters of discontent, seasons of ceaseless rain, could be graphed and quartered and undergo the hand of cartographers until the northern lights dim with exhaustion, still you might never appear in the incarnation i desire, the precise contour of resolve and steadfast sinew i seek to anchor my sororitas surges, my maternal imperatives, my infant divinations. are you hurricane or torrent, engineer's shovel or crane's lament? could gather your liquid rock till we can no longer tell ourselves apart, could suckle your raised ire until your thirst subsides, could wrap our spent bodies into the textures of igneous, sediment, underground streams until the crows and ravens chatter distress in suburban neighbourhoods, in hopes our porous husks feed hunters, gatherers, compassionate world-eaters

"i would rather unleash fire than have fire unleash me." — Richard Van Camp

References

Anderson, Laurie. "Walking and Falling." *Big Science*. Warner, 1982.

Benyus, Janine. *Biomimicry: Innovation Inspired by Nature*. New York: Harper Perennial, 2002.

Bhaggiyadatta, Krisantha Sri. *52nd State of Amnesia*. Toronto: TSAR, 1993.

Body Burden. Queyras, France, dir. 2000.

Darwish, Mahmoud. *Unfortunately, It Was Paradise: Selected Poems*. Berkeley: University of California Press, 2003.

Exporting Harm. Basel Action Network. 2002. http://www.ban.org.

Grossman, Elizabeth. *High Tech Trash: Digital Devices, Hidden Toxics, and Human Health*. Washington, DC: Island Press, 2006.

Frye, Northrop. *The Anatomy of Criticism*. Princeton: Princeton University Press, 1957.

Hassan, Marwan. *Velocities of Zero: Conquest, Colonization, and the Destruction of Cultures*. Toronto: TSAR, 2002.

Hawkes, David, trans. *Songs of the South: An Anthology of Ancient Chinese Poems by Qu Yuan and Other Poets*. New York: Penguin, 1985.

High, Kathy. "23 Questions." *Processed Lives: Gender and Technology in Everyday Life*. Eds. Jennifer Terry and Melodie Calvert. New York: Routledge, 1997.

Ho, Mae-wan. *Genetic Engineering: Dream or Nightmare?* New York: Continuum, 2000.

Hsu, Kai-Yu, trans. and ed. *Twentieth Century Chinese Poetry: An Anthology*. Ithaca, NY: Cornell Paperbacks, 1970. (includes poems by Ping Hsin, Wen I-to, Cheng Min, and much more)

Kiyooka, Roy. "October's Piebald Skies and Other Lacunae." *Pacific Windows: Collected Poems of Roy K. Kiyooka*. Ed. Roy Miki. Vancouver: Talonbooks, 1997.

Laduke, Winona. *Recovering the Sacred: The Power of Naming and Claiming*. Cambridge, MA: South End Press, 2005.

Lai, Larissa. *When Fox Is a Thousand*. Vancouver: Press Gang, 1995.

Laiwan. "Dirty laundry and clean technology: can computers ever be innocent?" 1 Feb. 2007. http://dpi.studioxx.org/index.php?id=103

Lew, Walter K. *Premonitions: The Kaya Anthology of New Asian North American Poetry*. New York: Kaya, 1995.

Meadows, Donella. "Leverage Points: Places to Intervene in a System." Sustainability Institute home page. 1999. http://www.sustainabilityinstitute.org/pubs/Leverage_Points.pdf

Newton, David. *The Chemical Elements*. New York: F. Watts, 1994.

Percy Schmeiser home page. http://www.percyschmeiser.com.

Pun, Ngai. *Made in China: Women Factory Workers in a Global Workplace*. Durham, NC: Duke UP, 2005.

Rich, Adrienne. "To invent what we desire." *What Is Found There: Notebooks on Poetry and Politics*. New York: Norton, 1994.

Ronell, Avital. *Crack Wars: Literature, Addiction, Mania*. Lincoln: University of Nebraska Press, 1992.

Rukeyser, Muriel. *Life of Poetry*. Ashfield, MA: Paris Press, 1996.

Sapir, Edward. "The Status of Linguistics as a Science." *Edward Sapir: Culture, Language and Personality*. Ed. David Mandelbaum. Berkeley: University of California Press, 1964.

Shiva, Vandana. *Biopiracy: The Plunder of Nature and Knowledge*. Toronto: Between the Lines, 1997.

Van Camp, Richard. *Angel Wing Splash Pattern*. Cape Croker Reserve, Wiarton, ON: Kegedonce Press, 2002.

Warshall, Peter. "Symbiosis." *Civil Disobediences: Poetics and Politics in Action*. Eds. Anne Waldman and Lisa Birman. Minneapolis: Coffee House Press, 2004. 137–59.

Uts'am. Witness. http://www.utsam-witness.ca/.

Photographs

Page 8: Interior of Victoria Rice Mills showing rice packaged in mats and Chinese worker, ca. 1889. Credit: Robert Wilson Redford and family fonds/PA-118183. Source: Library and Archives Canada

Page 24: Worker Agnes Wong of Whitecourt, Alberta, assembles a sten gun produced for China by the Small Arms Ltd. plant, Long Branch, ON, April, 1944. Source: Library and Archives Canada. Credit: Ronny Jacques, National Film Board of Canada. Still Photography Division. PA-108043

Page 78: On the corner of 18th and Prince Edward, Saltwater City. Photograph by Henry Tsang.

Acknowledgements

Most of this manuscript was written on Coast Salish land, and I would like to acknowledge the Tsleil Watuth (Burrard), XwMuthkwium (Musqueam) and Skxwúmish (Squamish) Nations on whose territoriès I have lived and worked for many years. I also owe a debt to the Tsuu Tina (Sarcee), Siksika (Blackfoot), and Stoney First Nations, whose territories intersect around Calgary, where I was born and raised. This past year, I have also lived in Miami, the lands of the Miccosukee, Seminole, Tequesta, and Calusa peoples.

With love & gratitude to my family & communities: Canace & Peter Wong; Cindy, Jeff & Luke; Pat & Billiejo; the large clan of Chans (including the resilient, rambunctious twins Tania & Miranda) and Wongs; Walter, Hiromi, Larissa, Roy, Ashok, Eva, Jenny, Agnes, Susanda, Michelle, Lily, Linda, Baco, Grace, Cindy, Shirley, Dorothy, Eloginy, Angeline, Shane, Lydia, Eileen, Ritz, Ivana, Donna, Ritchie, Weyman, Glen, Karolle, Randy, Henry, all my daring comrades (Direct Action Against Refugee Exploitation), and more. Roy Miki, Larissa Lai, Hiromi Goto, and Michael Barnholden's encouragement and feedback especially contributed to this manuscript's momentum. Hiromi's and Larissa's astute observations and senses of humour, along with sweet mackerel dinners, have sustained me over many difficult times. For insightful edits, intimate witness and squirrelly joy, I thank Walter K. Lew.

Over the years, I've been fortunate to participate in IntraNations' exciting projects, Interdisciplinary Forums at the Emily Carr Institute, discussions and readings at the Kootenay School of Writing. My life has been changed by DARE and Joint Effort's visits to women in prison. More activities and gatherings that have fed this manuscript's process: Imagining Asian and Native Women: Deconstructing from

Contact to Modern Times – organized by Lee Maracle; Dionne Brand's workshop at Booming Ground; a retreat guided by Olga Broumas; a Reconnecting to Life workshop led by Jackie Larkin and Maggie Ziegler; the Poetry, Pedagogy, and Internationalisms Conference; the Crisis of the Political Colloquium; the Hong Kong International Literary Festival; Trans-Scribing Canada: Canadian Writers in Taiwan; Alley Alley Home Free: A North American Poetry and Poetics Conference and Festival in Honour of Pauline Butling and Fred Wah; the Renegotiating Identities Conference in Australia; the PSU Feminisms Conference "Looking Back, Moving Forward;" travels in Germany with Glen Lowry and Larissa Lai; the Powell Street Festival; Under the Volcano; and more.

Parts of this manuscript were written and edited in the refuge of Evelina M. Galang's home, in the company of Chaconito and Lake Osceola. I feel blessed by the students and colleagues I've encountered and befriended at the Emily Carr Institute in Vancouver and at the University of Miami. Thanks to Sandra Semchuk and Laiwan for critical thought and for helping with earlier versions of the cover, to Sita Kumar for generously and diligently taking author photographs. Silas White has been a very patient and thorough editor.

Poems from this manuscript have previously appeared in chapbooks produced by Roy Miki entitled *present imperfect, nervous organism,* and *restless bodies;* in journals such as *West Coast Line, Ms, filling Station, Open Letter, Stylus Poetry Journal, Massachusetts Review, XCP (Cross-Cultural Poetics), Rice Paper, Slant, Columbia Poetry Review, Prairie Fire, Windsor ReView; dANDelion, Alphabet City, Canadian Literature; Capilano Review, parser;* and in the following anthologies: *The Common Sky: Canadian Writers Against the War, Making a Difference: Canadian Multicultural Literatures in English, Shift and Switch: New Canadian Poetry, Companions and Horizons: an Anthology of SFU Poetry; Portfolio Milieu;* and *Swallowing Clouds: An Anthology of Chinese-Canadian Poetry.*

The writing of this manuscript was made possible with the support of a Canada Council creative writing grant, Canada Council travel grants, and a Social Sciences and Humanities Research Council doctoral fellowship.

ABOUT THE AUTHOR

Rita Wong's first book, *monkeypuzzle*, was published by Press Gang in 1998. A recipient of the Asian Canadian Writers' Workshop Emerging Writer Award, Wong is an assistant professor in the Critical + Cultural Studies department at the Emily Carr Institute in Vancouver and a visiting instructor at the University of Miami.

In 1963, bill bissett founded blewointmentpress in Vancouver and began publishing mimeographed magazines of experimental poetry. Within a few years bissett, known for his own work in sound and concrete poetry, began to publish books that subversively extended the boundaries of language, visual image and political statement, including work by bpNichol, Steve McCaffery, Andrew Suknaski, Lionel Kearns & d.a. levy. Meeting wide acclaim and controversy, the activities of blewointmentpress have had a seminal influence on the Canadian literary community.

After a drastic reduction in government support in 1982, the press stuggled with debt and bissett sold blewointment. It was renamed Nightwood Editions by Maureen Cochrane & David Lee. After a couple more incarnations of the press moving bissett-like back and forth across the country and publishing work as diverse as poetry, fiction, film & music criticism and children's titles, Nightwood launched a "blewointment" imprint in 2005 to honour bissett and the press's innovative and political roots.

blewointment titles available from Nightwood Editions:

False Maps for Other Creatures/ Jay MillAr/ poetry/ 978-0-88971-203-4 5.25 x 8.5/ 96 pp/ $16.95/ 2005

radiant danse uv being: a poetic portrait of bill bissett/ edited by Jeff Pew & Stephen Roxborough/ anthology/ 978-0-88971-210-2 8.5 x 9.5/ 172 pp/ paper/ $23.95/ b&w illustrations/ 2006

Hitch/ Matthew Holmes/ poetry/ 978-0-88971-214-0/ $16.95/ paper/ 5.25 x 8.75/ 80 pp/ 2006

Birch Split Bark/ Diane Guichon/ poetry/ 978-0-88971-215-7/ $16.95/ paper 5.5 x 8.5/ 104 pp/ 2007

forage/ Rita Wong/ poetry/ 978-0-88971-213-3/ $16.95/ paper/ 5.5 x 8 88 pp/ 2007

For more information on these titles please browse:
www.nightwoodeditions.com. Prices subject to change.